steps and stories

Heidi Davies

a book of dreamer's disease
for those fascinated by a life of movement

for those who dream

As the seasons change and the world moves around us, something is always changing within us too. No matter what path we choose, what footsteps we take: we are all just stories, connections, journeys, movements - forever evolving. We are all somehow part of every single person we've ever met in our life, all part of every place we've ever been.
We are all full of stories worth telling. Connections... however big or small - they make this life beautiful.

every footstep
holds the power
to unearth
new worlds within
and tell a story
step
after step
stories
upon stories

and so write
just write
let your dreams
take flight

once upon a time
there was
a young girl
full of words
with no way
to release
or unfasten
the torrent
of sentences
from her spirit
but then
this young girl
she found
her gift
when she moved
she could be anything
when she moved
she became
the writing
when she moved
she became
the dreams
the dreamer
she was unleashed
she was unstoppable

the simple
magic
of everyday
waves
ripples
endless blue
wild
wonderful
dreams
stay true

the excitement
lacing up
your trainers
wondering where
your feet
will take you
today
the anticipation
suddenly
you're out there
floating
on silent strides
nothing else matters
you're free
you're alive
you're running
there's no greater
gift
no greater
feeling
i fall in love
every time

words
seem to just
have the ability
to spill
out of me
they don't come
from my head
or from my mind
writing is more
an unconscious process
something i feel
bubble up
from deep
inside of me
words
rattling the bars
of their cages
demanding
to be released
written down
ink on paper
ideas
thoughts
passions
hopes

dreams
sometimes so many
seem to brim up
from my being
and i simply
cannot write
fast enough
my pen
cannot keep up
with my energy within
i like that

running into
nothingness
with something
like wholeness
deep inside
wet
cold
wild
but alive

the wild of my mind
often recalls
time
moments
memories
i thought
i'd left behind

nature may have
the ability
to chill my bones
but
it will always
keep my heart
warm

one could say
i have
a head
full of elsewhere
my head
in the clouds

free
like a bird
floating
on the wind
playing
with the currents
in the sky
let them
wonder why

swim through challenge
stay afloat
know your ocean
own it
now
you must trust
in the mood
of waves

from tiny
seeds
grow mighty
trees

through
below
beneath
get out
of your own way

mountains climbed
valleys below
paths followed
rocks
gathered
held
messy and true
unfolding stories
making up
every part of you

18

something scares you?
good
that means you're living
acknowledge your fear
feel it
the anticipation
the hammering of your heart
beating audibly in your ears
sweaty palms
dry mouth
adrenaline
shooting through your veins
embrace your fear
fright
flight
or fight
you decide
choose wisely

sometimes
you cannot
be big
and bold
like the sun
for everyone
to see

sometimes
you can
only be
still
and silent

dormant embers
ash
glowing
ready
to burn

patiently
you must wait
for elements
like oxygen
like inspiration

your passions
will burn
burn
alight
gloriously
a wildfire
once more

                              warmth
                     the way the sun
                              sets
                           dapples
                    across the land
                           golden
                      the colour
                         of dry
                   blissful sand

here one minute
gone the next
like the summer

                              autumn
                          tap tap
                        tapping
                 on the window

22

what matters
is now
and not then
you
and not them
build your own
castles
in the sand
there are already
castles
deep inside
your bones

you know
it's actually
kind of very okay
not to know
yet
the beauty is often
in the discovery
the journey

courage above fear
and you will
be unstoppable
my dear

i've grown weary
of acting strong
it feels all wrong
it's somewhere right now
i don't belong
i am weak
self-love
and courage
are what i seek
i crumble
but i will
reassemble
piece by piece
a jigsaw
furiously unravelling
set to
mend

and whilst it's true
none of these paths
lead you safely back
to who
you used to be
like a river
changing currents
building
strengthening with motion
tributaries of
your past self
flowing
into something
whole
raw
pure and true
a river
this is you

the things
that make you
feel lit up
and alive
sensing
the sun
from the inside
out
you should do more
of these things
don't shrink
shine

you said
i was floating
a cardboard box
soggy
in the ocean
but now
i've found
my motion
i hold
my own oar
i've chosen
to guide myself
go my own way
onwards
but never
to the shallow shore

if you were
to take a trip
to the supermarket
with a lengthy shopping list
of your daily essentials
forget it
ignore the milk
and the bread
instead
smile at the stranger
perhaps stood
in a bitter quandary
over reduced french stick
or their routine wholemeal
let them realise
it does not matter
it's just bread
food all the same
instead what matters
what we require
on our shopping list
the daily essentials
above the milk and bread
above the confusion
of bursting bargain shelves

are things like
love
kindness
passion
these irreplaceable connections
these are
priceless
a smile and a nod
from the stranger
their daily essentials
are imminent

through the fog
searching for sun
the best way out
is always
through

flying
without even trying
dear gravity
you won't ever
bring me back
down to earth
because now
i know
my own
worth
i'm soaring
above the clouds
leaving
my doubts
my fears
behind

there are so many
bright windows
of great opportunity
right in front
of your eyes
if only
you have
the courage
to look
and see

if i stop
pause
and think back
back to when
i was a young child
i feel the warmth
of my childhood days
stretch out before my eyes
and i feel so thankful
for the life of love and happiness
i have around me
for family give you the roots
to hold yourself
still and steady
in an ever-changing
and unpredictable world
but also the branches
to grow
to flourish
to be whoever and whatever
you wish to be
in a world
of a thousand
different coloured leaves
a million possibilities

you think
you were not
born for adventure
but do you not
remember
how as a child
you wanted to touch everything
feel
the earth around you
jump
in the deepest puddles
reach up high
to sit
on your fathers' shoulders
just so you could survey
the world
from a different space

don't tell me
you're not an adventurer
when we both know
deep down
this is who we are
the human experience

changing perceptions
moving
growing
being

feed your wild
dear child

seeking
the purpose
striving
for this passion
spin
wobble
balance
all you have
to do
is begin
start somewhere
happiness
begins
here
in ordinary life
you will bloom
as you are

first footsteps
infinite possibilities
the gift of movement
is a seed
it grows
and remains
for life

why must you wear a frown
on a rainy day?
the cool sensation
of dampness
penetrating your skin
is surely a reminder
you're here
on this planet
you're alive

a firey ball
of ash and dust
orbiting
in the vast stillness
of space
souls fill
with complete awe
at this magnificence
that we be so lucky
to be here
right now
alive

the rain may pitter
or patter

down your window pane
the window
the border
or perhaps the space
between you
and the rest
of the galaxy
between you
and your wildest dreams

don't let the water
falling from
the darkened sky
stop you
you're here
right now
alive

being
out in nature
unlocks so much
from deep inside of me
thoughts
words
feelings
emotions
the beauty of
the natural world
is literally the key
to my soul
so take me to nature
and witness my being
rejoice and smile
at the wilderness around
and unearth
open up
a new world within

the low
familiar call
of the pigeon
suddenly
i'm five again
waking up
in the family campervan
morning
and the day spans out
life stretches on
i'm young
full of wonder
awe
possibility
now
the pigeon
my heart
still free
endlessly

those
jagged
missing parts
are waiting
slowly
slowly
to be filled
soon
you will be
so full
overflowing
with love
with life
if only
you continue
to remain
open
to the good

own who you are
but do not be afraid
if you don't quite know
who that is
just yet
be open to
your changing tides
and flow
you are human
raw
and oh so
powerful

maybe there is a pathway
for each and every one of us
a destiny yet to be fulfilled
one day you'll trip and stumble
onto your greatest revelation
and suddenly everything will magically
make sense
you'll calm your hammering heart
breathe deeply
exhaling the tightened knots of worry
that have had their arms grasped
tightly
around your lungs for so long
the questions unanswered
will finally be understood
and you'll come to realise
you shouldn't question after all
because no matter what happens
whether you ask or not
doors will always open
and life will always answer
embrace the confusion embrace fear
and let the path reveal itself
for even in the deepest darkest forests
there is still a way through

smell of sweet bracken
on a warm
summer's day
transports me back
to my childhood
wandering
hills
country lanes
family
by my side
smiles
laughter
weary limbs
forward motion
towards home

the moments
that dwarf us

vast horizons
reaching out
stretching
in every direction
the wind
wildly
immensely
powerful

listen
nature
does not wish
to be silenced

i love those dark autumn nights
the light of day melts away
and the purple-blue of dusk
encompasses the sky
the wind
the whoosh of air
through the dry autumn leaves
silent ominous clouds
rolling overhead
the promise of tomorrow's rain
hanging like a question mark in the air
the in-betweens
day, dusk, night
sun, endless cloud, stormy rain
today, now, tomorrow
walk through the shadowy autumn
gloom
and ride your storms

these windy days
i treasure
air swells
and swirls
unhindered
a fine dance
a daring act
aliveness
is a grand thing
freely lionhearted
wild
like the wind

every fibre of your being
can sing
and hum
with aliveness
if only
you let it
you have the power
to open
to deepen
to orchestrate
your life
making every note
your own
compose
your symphony
conduct
the harmony
those who are ready
to listen
will witness
you glisten
and rise
to a crescendo
on your wave
of sound beside you

i sit
pen in hand
scribbling down
random thoughts
the world map
below
my notebook
the never ending
atlas
foreign lands
not yet explored
mountains
yet to be climbed
and experienced
my whole life
ahead of me
this
an incredible freedom
humbling
overwhelming
there is so much
gratitude
for everything
places already visited
paths already traveled

friendships already made
the connections
and the journey
now
the world
it is waiting
for me
and
for you too

i believe in fairies
hiding down
at the bottom
of the garden
daintily dancing
among the wildflowers
along with
a unicorn
living in the shed
you don't have to imagine
these things
to know they're real
just believe
a pinch
of magic
take it
with a pinch
of salt

the small moments
between
footsteps
where life begins
and where it ends
discover
somewhere to run to
escape
where the connections
are free
we are not confined
to this time
the edges are interwoven
into every part of you
i crave this groove
i need to move
infinitely

build your own
castles in the air
towers of your dreams
sky high
ocean wide
let your thoughts
wander off
the edge
of the earth
there's no map for this
the fortress
of your imagination
is boundless
unique
and pure

sometimes
my twenty year old self
can't bear it
the dull ache
locked in my chest
a longing
for what's to come
the future
so vast
so full
the magic pull
of the open road
i have to go
the present
leaves me weary

i've been thinking lately
how home isn't a place
not really
four walls, bricks, cement
may build a house
but it doesn't make it home
home is a feeling
deep inside every one of us
wholeness
something clicking neatly into place
being content
comfortable with oneself
now in this moment
you are enough
you are made of stardust
and have the ability
to move mountains
to start fires within
no matter where you stand
on this planet
you will never be homeless
if only you understand
the revelation
being at home
starts from within

why do you
bury
your head
deep in the sand
trailing
yourself back
pretending
to be normal
feigning order
when you're really
an avalanche
of gushing multitudes
please just
colour
outside
of the lines
the box
is so much
more
than
all this
apply all
your crayons

not in nature
simply
part of mother nature
an unspoken alliance
built
with these tall trees
a deep understanding
swerving
along the path
flying
on silent strides
breathing
in damp
fresh
wood-like air

stop
halt
simply
take a moment
survey
this spectacle
your flesh
body and mind
a tiny speck
in the enormity
of the universe
these moments
you live for
you are
untamed
like nature
moving together
in harmony

you taught me
patience
is a virtue
a lesson
i cherish
like the cloth
in my ears
time marches on
the ever-moving
continuous
tick tock
of the clock
pedalling backwards
to conker filled days
teasels
on the common
encouraging
our fidgety
young fingers
to pick up
the pencils
and draw
create
whatever our mind
wandered to

our pencils
will move
evermore
across the page
because of you
memories
moments
forever treasured
we miss you
and all the spaces
where
you should have been
all the places
where
you are seen
time marches on
but you're still here
in our patient steps
everyday
the bells
ring on

there is strength
in waiting
courage
in silence
dreams
in depths
truths
in time

snailing around
it's all there
somewhere
just waiting
to be found

longing for change
the way
the sticky heat of summer
longs for
the downpour of rain

tall trees
falling leaves
autumn breeze

the slow
slip away of heat
softness
lightness
candyfloss clouds
the shades
of the setting sun
beauty is always present
it just
takes on
a multitude
of different forms
here
now
forever
always

slowly but surely
the heat of summer
slips away
and the autumnal chill
serves as a gentle reminder
things are forever changing
but there's so much beauty
in the unknown
the days and moments ahead
go live it

autumn sun
peeping
through the gap
at the top
of the curtains

golden

a reminder
you are
too

the hesitation
between summer
and autumn
balance
lightly lightly
across
the tightropes
of time
come
don't be timid
leaves
will soon bring
an easy landing
if you were
to fall
lightly lightly
tiptoe across
the expanses
of time

slowly
and then all at once
a sky full
of wonder
reaching out
the horizons
yonder

something special
about september sunsets
autumn
tapping on the window
the lingering light

71

october
the autumn wizard
casting spells
luminous sparks
specks of golden light
unmistakable
within all this grey
let the leaves
tumbling around you
remind you
it is essential
and necessary
to let things go
whirlwinds of colour
fascinating changes
shifts in time

two pairs of gloves
shuffling
over these hills
i love
but still
time to linger
means
frozen fingers
reaching out
cold hands
distant lands

if you're happy
and you know it
no matter
where you are
jump
jump to the stars

i don't know
if i need writing
or if writing
needs me
it's a seagull
hovering high
above the shore
never far away
my pen
demands me to stay
often i don't know
what i think
until it's written
with ink
i don't try to understand
but instead i trust
the same way i presume
my heart to beat
unconsciously free

just a speck

.

a dot
in the vastness
of it all

like pebbles
we are all
small
our assorted diversity
distinct
and pure
yes
we are all
vital
the whole
shore

we all have those days
we wish could last forever
moments we turn back to
in our minds' eye
living the memory
as if the memories were made only
yesterday
those fleeting
days of wonder
will live on
always
because you remember

the trouble is
we're all far too
"busy"
to understand
what silence
and stillness
really mean
so go on
i urge you
sit
just be
as you are
for at least one moment
you may discover why
"busy"
leaves your soul
feeling dead
and why
stillness
gifts you
with
oh-so much
movement
an opening

in my mind
i run and run
run wild and free
there are no boundaries
all i feel is the aliveness
and freedom
that come with being able to dream

pitter patter
mind over matter

i've been spending my days
hopping on one leg
supported by two sticks
hoping with my head in the clouds
supported by my dreams
maybe the differences
do not outweigh the similarities
don't try to run
before you can walk
you will only
fall deeper
but you have the strength
to climb
maybe if you look
you will see
a correlation between
hopping and hoping
hopping and dreaming
spending my days hopping
has given me more time
to ponder
more time to wonder
will i sink or swim
fall or rise
frown or smile

weaker or stronger
the beauty is that i get to decide
and i choose gratitude over grievance
almost nearly every time
but do not be fooled
there are moments
when the darkness creeps up on me
and i forget
for a moment
my head spins
and worry tightens
knots in my stomach
i forget how to breathe
i wonder if it will ever
be the same again
i remind myself
it will not be the same
it will be better
more understanding
influence
inspiration
illumination
gratitude
all is well
because i breathe

missing the way
movement
makes me feel
being alive
out in the countryside
just my footsteps
my dreams
and imagination
for company
that flow
and energy
pure-state
childlike wonder
it gifts me

some days i miss running
a little extra
struggle to find ways
to fill the gaps
but the light
at the end
looms brighter
feelings
a little
lighter

you're going
to make it
but even
if you don't
know that the act
of trying
is enough
you can
be tough
rest
don't stress
why not
begin again
tomorrow
try
just try
it's okay
to cry
maybe you'll learn
how to smile
through your tears
try
try again
in spite
of your fears

find your fire
glowing
and yes
then you'll
always
be growing
no matter
where you are
just look
to the stars

these days of stillness
leave me restless
i crave
the duet
of sweet fatigue
between gasping breaths
and pounding feet
the fluidity of movement
using my legs
as a means
of exploration
opening my heart
to the unknown
to the paths
and mountains
before me
for now i am stuck
instead i let
the words and memories
wash around me
cascading
like a waterfall
these words
and moments
draw me back

to the simple balance
of recovery
healing
this is the new focus
time
marches on
i am still
but my mind
oh
how it runs

the moments and occasions
where the light shines through
it all connects
eventually and continually
a wander at sunset
watching the light of day fade away
slowly
and then all at once
a smile and a kind word
shared with a neighbour or a stranger
in the street
a picnic
a road trip
a family meal and homegrown parsnips
roasted to perfection
laughter and a walk in the countryside
sharing dreams, passions, ideas
even from hundreds
of miles away
the inspiration
all around
your favourite books
a simple sunrise and candy floss clouds
a cat's meow and the purr of comfort
the music you love and feel

the way you can just
pick up your pen
and let
these thoughts
escape you
the sky
so vast and so full
cooking with your grandmother
the silence after rain
helping a child
grasp the concept
of using all their fingers
to dance
across the keys
of the piano

all this and more
simple
yet significant
this is life

the mountains
and the valleys
are adventures
alike

stillness
rattles at my edges
tears me to shreds
i know
i'm whole
as i am
i'm enough
movement
whispers to me
in my dreams
but for now
here
is enough
it's all enough
all the
glorious complexities
some revelations
dawn calmly
just breathe

some kind
of wonderful

dance across the surface of the world
we are all made
of dreams
we are all made
of the paths
we dare
to take
and
even the ones
we don't

dance
dance
because
you are free

the green tomato
bravely exists
patient
beside the shining red
we cannot remain
as we are
we must go on
move grow
red
green
shades in-between
remember
the pace of growth
is personal

runner beans
the way they grow
up
out
winding
spiraling
around the trellis
fascinating
loose stalks
pointing
like fingers
to light
to warmth

the plants
that grow
through concrete
trusting
the light
stretching
fighting
reaching out
to the sky
through the cracks
and dirt
born from
self-belief
the flower
does not ask
it just
blooms

the dwindling ebb
of who you are
is flowing away
on the breeze
trickling down-stream
into something
so much bigger
than all this
if you're waiting
for a sign
this
is it
your ocean
is waiting

music
a mechanism of time travel
an aching counterpoint
between what was
then
and what is
now
a light silvery cobweb
between past
and present
riding the wistful adventure
a random jumble of notes
surges of nostalgic harmony
the mixed-up magic
this is music

you
one so bold
look inside
unearth your
pot of gold

a band of colour
suspended
an arc
across the sky
a delightful sight
momentary
prisms of light

are you not ready
or are you
just scared
your subconscious
a lighthouse
keeping the danger
away
are you too busy
sailing
drifting backwards
to embark
on your voyage
your anchor
has been here
all along
you're made to travel
deep
not lost at sea
you're part
of these waves
so please
won't you
just
dive in

jazzed up
music
the world's getting smaller
i am feeling
a little warmer
with the beats
you gift me
though thousands
of miles away
the simplicity of the connection
is pure
geography
i know i'm often
wondering
about it
about you
more

books
pages unturned
adventures unseen
people
yet to meet
places
yet to visit
journeys
unfolding
at your fingertips
here
a dead tree
an adventure
open eyes
open hearts
libraries
of wonder
words
just the beginning

live
dream
the way you read
one page
at a time

discovering
how to
untangle
the messy webs
of adulthood
rather than
the wool
knotted
around
our trees
in the garden

together
it's better

when you feel something
bubble up
from deep inside of you
a feeling of
love
hope
passion
joy
the spark of a flame
you use to light
your fire
deep within your soul
use that energy
let it seep outwards
feel it
pulsing through your veins
buried deep
within your lungs
between the small spaces
the air you breathe
stirring the waves
deep in your belly
let yourself
be entirely consumed
by this passion

breathe it
inhale
exhale
live it
for life was never about
being cold or dark
find your rays
find your warmth
and be your light

we keep dreaming
with no limits
learning from
each other
the silences
and the stillness
the uncommon sensibility
we share
makes me wonder

isn't it wonderful
how you can travel and explore
go literally anywhere
breathe the air of new exciting and
exotic places
immerse yourself in unfamiliar cultures
and environments
chasing your curiosity
discovering limitless possibilities
all this
and yet i admit
here
at home
mid wales does something to me
i feel it's magic
deep in my bones

the mountains
that made me really go
something like
!!!!!!!!
on the inside
for the very
first time

it remains
evolving
sometimes blurred
hazy

sometimes immersed
fully focused
at the centre

whenever or whatever
it's enough just to feel it's there

nestled
deep in the valley
between the high peaks
waking to glimpse
the morning sun
jumping up
over the beautiful mountains
on the horizon
looking out
down to where
the magic happens
a feeling
of returning
warmth
felt deep
in my bones
this is where
i'm meant to be
i am at home

the sky
it has many layers
many clouds
before you reach
the shining sun

humans
in a way
are similar
don't let
the moody shrouds
eclipse
your light
your joy

life
is too short
to exist
in grey

be golden
go on
i know
you want to

go with me
somewhere
anywhere
come
let our feet
guide us
our souls
will lead us
to the mountains
and onwards
up
to the stars

do you notice
if you hold
onto silence
some people
can't help
but try
to fill it up
but listen
really listen
silence
has harmony
sweet chords
you don't always
have to make noise
to feel
a melody

lusting after
verticality
moving between
rocky
jagged peaks
a head
in the clouds
gazing
at the
blue expanse
of tranquil water
below
zooming out
from where i was
crawling ants
a stark contrast
mountains
magnified
my whole body
in the clouds
on this peak
seeing
just breathing
believing

you know
it's just
a mountain
state of mind

letting go
is the art
of holding onto yourself
more
you are already enough
as you are
life is beautiful
it's here and now
and the goal
is not to become
what the world
wants you to be
but to be more
of who you are
and what you dream of becoming

take me
to where
the land
meets
the sky
let's
gaze
up
at the rooftops
of the world
full of wonder

the mountains
are moving
always
and us too
here
along this journey
alive
loving
living
then
now
and forever

time
four letters
a continuous eternity
do what you can
with what you have

everyone is on a journey
sometimes the path
isn't so clear
you need
a little helping hand
from the people
around you
ultimately
everything is connected
we can grow
and flourish
by lifting others
that is what
makes us human
this is what
makes life wonderful

if you feel
like you can
make a tiny
difference
to even just
one persons' life
then that
is enough
we are all
here
we all
matter
tiny differences
add up
it all matters
everything

the only
permanent thing
in this life
is change
and so
embrace it
enjoy
wherever you are
right now
and allow yourself
to grow
through the spaces
the gaps
the in-betweens
even in all your difficulties
you are still
blooming

imagine
imagine
be a doer
be a dreamer
hold onto
your vision
clasp it
here
in the palms
of your hands

we run
up high
into the mountains
with the setting sun
casting long shadows
over the earth
we run
swapping stories
adventures
in other lands
we run
sometimes
in blissful silence
mesmerised
by the rocky giants
above us
below us
within us
the marmots
whistle
and our hearts
pound
bodies sing
the continual hum
of aliveness

tearing down
the single track
descending as fast
as your body
and the laws
of physics will allow
limbs
a tangle
of blurring
momentum
wind
rushing
in your ears
eyes
streaming
tears
of sheer velocity
tears
of happiness
closer
and closer
to flying
never feeling
so alive

moving swiftly
dancing over the terrain
laughing with amusement
a gleeful
sense of wonder
monumental
mouthfuls of joy
escaping your lips
filling
the eerie silence
encompassing the forest
scattering the notes
you are
the conductor
of this marvelous
created kingdom
soaring
on pure raw
human emotion
senses
activated
to the highest
heights
this is real

nine years old
back in school
pen to paper
scrawling stories
it was forbidden to end this way
i'm sorry teacher
now i cannot prevent
this unlikely turn of events

the gentle constant rhythm
raindrops
drumming on the window
an enchanting harmony
lulling me out of the door

the gentle constant rhythm
my feet
pitter patter
my hammering heart
allegro - the pace in my chest
a splash and a splosh
leaping oceans of puddles
the sea in my shoes
a stream
ebbing from my head

down to the very tip
of my toes
dripping down my nose

red raw hands
sodden sticky clothes
a new layer of skin
where does the rain stop
and where do i begin

the gentle constant rhythm
a feeling
- blissfully alive
i'm sorry teacher
but for now this is true
there's nothing i can do

i woke up

it was all a dream

dark times
do come
they are in fact
inevitable
a reminder
the light
it can
be found
you are
strong
enough
and you are
brave
enough
as you are
you are
enough

life is huge
we shouldn't try
to understand it
just live it
make the most
of every moment
and be
insanely
grateful

yesterday
was international
mountain day
but there's no cure
for the disease
of the dreamers
the everyday dance
of the high peaks
roaming
across the mind

life goes on
movement and motion
running continues
writing - the pen's
journey
across the page
these things
never ending
pitter patter
the catalyst
for these
daydreaming
stories
twenty years young
a journey
adventure
only just
begun
dreamer's disease
will never
drift away
dreaming
is here
to stay

dreamers
the universe
is yours
your mountain
is waiting
step out
onto the path
write
your stories

About the author:

Heidi Davies grew up in the heart of Mid Wales, surrounded by the rolling hills with the call of nature around every corner.

She has been running ever since she was ten years old in all sorts of races. Track, cross country, road running...

In 2014 her heart was stolen by the hills and her main focus switched to the somewhat challenging but wholly invigorating sport of mountain running.

Mountain running has opened up Heidi's eyes to the world and the natural environment in which we live and the many different possibilities. The different cultures, languages and the numerous breathtakingly beautiful places you get to run. She finds herself craving future adventures and continuously looking forward to where her feet may take her next. Ultimately, Heidi runs because exploring new places by foot makes her happy.

Mountain running is so much more than just a sport. It's about the inspiring people you meet, the incredible places you get to visit, the close friendships you build and the unforgettable memories you make. It's so much more than a run up a hill.

The sport of mountain running has led Heidi home. Now she lives in Italy in the magical town of Malonno. The country of the mountain race. Here mountain running is embedded deep into the history of the town. The tradition of the FlettaTrail race is ingrained into the spirit of the people and the crisp mountain air. Heidi's first experience of the race in 2017 led her to dream of making Malonno her home... and now here she is. Heidi can't get enough of the mountains, the tall trees and simple things. She is spellbound by this magical place and the life here.

Heidi has always been passionate about movement and the body's ability to move through different landscapes whilst simultaneously creating thoughts and words along the way. Every footstep holds the ability to open up new worlds within and tell a story.

If you enjoyed this book, would you consider helping me by:
- Leaving a review on Amazon.
- Sharing a photo of this book on social media. Use the hashtag #stepsandstories.
- Giving your copy to someone who might benefit from reading it.

If you'd like to keep in touch you can:
- Follow me on Instagram: @heididavies98
- Visit thepianorunner.blogspot.com to read more of my personal stories and thoughts

Thank you fellow dreamers. May this book be a reminder to chase after your dreams and inspire you to find the mindful magic in everyday.

Be you, bravely.

Head over to the next page to read an extract from Heidi's next book, coming soon...

Monday 16th December 2019

"she believed she could, so she did"

For my 21st birthday at the start of the year, my parents gave me a bracelet. Engraved on it are the words "she believed she could, so she did" In the dark and in the light, these words have travelled with me everyday. These words have guided me forward along my journey, no matter where I've been... Wales, Italy, America, Patagonia and all the other places in-between. On my wrist I have a constant reminder of my strength - even when I have felt weak. And in my heart I have a constant reminder of my parents love - no matter how far apart we are. My parents and family have given me the roots - the strength to hold myself still and steady in an ever-changing and unpredictable world but also the branches to grow and to flourish. To be whoever and whatever I wish to be. If only I'm brave enough to believe...

Because...

I was lost. I was so lost... climbing through the dark forests of my mind. The walls I built myself. The restrictions I placed on my body. The box I put myself into. There seemed to be no way out. I was well and truly stuck. I had no strength to climb out. No energy. Limbs of lead and a mind of dread.

Now I can look back and smile at what I thought I wanted. The stupidity of the life I was living. The guilt, the shame. The constant comparison. Now I look back and remember most of all, just how constantly *hungry* I felt. That isn't anyway to live a life. That isn't any way to exist. There is so much more to life than the shape of your body. What matters most is the shape of your mind.

Maybe I didn't go through all that for nothing. Maybe it's a chapter of my story that I'm ashamed of... but it's still part of the book. Without it I wouldn't be me. Without it I wouldn't now be so free.

I was running on empty...

Cover Image in collaboration with Luke's Photography @lukesphotography05
Author Photo by Marco Gulberti @corsainmontagna.it

Printed in Great Britain
by Amazon

12878803R00081